Beautiful Ballerinas

By Heidi Adelman

www.childsworld.com

Published in the United States of America by The Child's World®
1980 Lookout Drive • Mankato, MN 56003-1705
800-599-READ • www.childsworld.com

ACKNOWLEDGMENTS

The Child's World®: Mary Berendes, Publishing Director

Produced by Shoreline Publishing Group LLC
President / Editorial Director: James Buckley, Jr.
Designer: Tom Carling, carlingdesign.com
Cover Design: Slimfilms

Photo Credits
Cover–Corbis (main); iStock, dreamstime (insets)
Interior–AP/Wide World: 21; Corbis: 6, 7, 13, 14, 18, 22, 24, 25, 26;
dreamstime.com: 12, 16, 17, 19; Getty Images 23; iStock: 5, 9, 11;
Courtesy Joffrey Ballet: 28; Photos.com: 15, 29.
.

LIBRARY OF CONGRESS CATALOG-IN-PUBLICATION DATA

Adelman, Heidi.
  Beautiful ballerinas / by Heidi Adelman.
    p. cm. — (Reading rocks!)
  Includes index.
  ISBN-13: 978-1-59296-863-3 (library bound : alk. paper)
  ISBN-10: 1-59296-863-5 (library bound : alk. paper)
 1. Ballet—Juvenile literature. 2. Ballet dancers—Juvenile
literature. I. Title. II. Series.

GV1787.5.A33 2007
792.8—dc22

2007004189

CONTENTS

4 CHAPTER 1
All About the Ballet

10 CHAPTER 2
Becoming a
Ballerina

20 CHAPTER 3
Famous Ballerinas

30 GLOSSARY

31 FIND OUT MORE

32 INDEX

ALL ABOUT THE Ballet

Have you ever been to the **ballet**? When you sit in the theater watching the beautiful dancers, it can feel as if you're in a magical place. There might be colorful costumes and lovely **scenery**. They can make you imagine you're visiting a faraway place or time in the past.

Ballerinas play the roles of princesses or swans or fairies or pretty country girls. They can also play animals or even monsters! They move in ways that most people can't. When ballerinas

dance, they often look as if they're floating or flying through the air. They keep perfect balance while they spin without becoming dizzy. They dance on the tips of their toes.

These young ballerinas are learning by watching other dancers on stage.

Italian ballerina Maria Taglioni models what ballerinas wore in the late 1800s.

Today, there are usually more ballerinas than there are male dancers in most ballets. But in the beginning, ballet was performed only by men. Men who were especially small or young played the roles of women. Women were not allowed to dance on stage. People thought it wasn't polite for women to show themselves off in public.

The first time a woman appeared in a **professional** ballet performance was 1685. Still, men continued to dance in most of the roles until the 1800s. That's when the long, heavy ballet costumes got lighter and shorter, and the women started to take center stage.

Ballet Beginnings

The word "ballet" is really a French word. That's because ballet was developed in the 1600s in France. King Louis XIV loved to dance so much that he hired his own dancing teacher. He also started the first school to train professional dancers.

Sometimes a ballet just expresses the way music makes people feel. But most of the time, a ballet tells a story. In the 1800s, **choreographers** (kor-ee-OG-ra-fers) began to make bigger and more difficult ballets that told complex stories. Story ballets were often about a man and woman who were in love. In these story ballets, women were usually the most important characters.

At about the same time, women learned to dance in new ways. They began to dance on the tips of their toes. This made it easier for them to spin and to look as if they could float like fairies. They also started wearing lighter, smaller costumes that allowed them to move more easily and gracefully.

Soon, all the most famous ballets had ballerinas as the main characters. It became the job of the male dancers to show off the ballerinas.

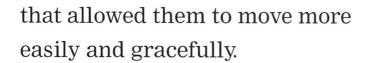

This ballerina practices one of her most important moves, dancing on the tips of her toes.

BECOMING A Ballerina

It takes many years of training to become a ballerina. Most dancers start taking lessons before they are 10, often at a ballet school in their hometown. But as they become teenagers, they **audition** for schools run by professional ballet companies. More than a thousand students might audition, but just a few hundred are accepted to join the school.

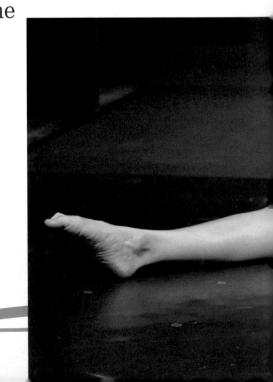

For many dancers, going to ballet school means living away from home. An average student might dance at ballet school, work at a part-time job, and take some classes to finish high school. There's not much time left over for hanging out with friends and having fun.

Sometimes, students get to dance in special holiday performances put on by the ballet company.

*Dancers must stretch out their muscles before each **rehearsal** or performance.*

This dancer is practicing her leaps. This move is called a jete *(zhe-TAY).*

When a dance student graduates from ballet school, her goal is to be accepted as a member of a professional ballet company. Some dancers are chosen from special summer-school programs. Other dancers go straight from ballet school into a professional company. But most dancers must begin auditioning for companies around the country—and sometimes around the world.

It's all part of looking for a job in the ballet business.

Many ballerinas start out by dancing with a small company. As they continue to perform well, they are noticed by larger companies. Most ballerinas have danced with several companies over their careers.

Do You Speak French?

Since ballet was developed in France, we use a lot of French words to talk about it. For example, a dance between two people, usually a man and a woman, is called a *pas de deux* (pah-duh-DOO). A glide is called a *glissade* (glee-SAHD). Even the little skirt a ballerina wears, the tutu, comes from the French word *tulle* (TOOL), which means a stiff fabric.

Most ballerinas start out in the *corps de ballet* (KOR duh bal-LAY)—that's a French term for the dancers in a ballet company who perform as a group. Sometimes they have a lot to do, and sometimes they form beautiful backgrounds for the star dancers.

As ballerinas gain confidence and show that they can take on more difficult roles, they become featured dancers. These dancers appear in small but special parts, sometimes

in groups of a few people (and sometimes dancing by themselves).

A single dancer performs dances called "solos."

Some featured dancers eventually become **principal dancers**, who are the stars of the ballet company. They perform alone on stage, or in front of all the other dancers. The most famous stars are the prima ballerinas. "Prima" means first—they're at the top!

A normal day for a ballerina is busy and difficult. She wakes up at about 7 o'clock in the morning and has a good breakfast. She takes classes from 8 o'clock to 10 o'clock to keep herself strong and **flexible**.

From 10 o'clock in the morning until 5 o'clock in the evening, she is in rehearsals with her ballet company. Then she might have an hour to go home and have dinner. She must be back at the theater by about 6 in the evening to warm up. Then it's time to put on her makeup and her costume.

From about 8 o'clock to 10 o'clock in the evening

Many ballet classes are designed to strengthen and tone muscles.

is the magical time when a ballerina is on stage, amazing everyone with her grace and beauty.

After the performance, she hangs up her costume, takes off her make-up, and heads home. A ballerina is usually in bed by 11:30 or midnight. That's a long day!

Like most performers, ballerinas use makeup to help create the characters they play.

Paloma Herrera (left) is from Argentina, while Marcelo Gomes (right) is from Brazil. Both dance for the popular American Ballet Theater.

Today, ballet is international. There are ballet companies in almost every country and in many cities. At the biggest ballet companies, the dancers come from all over the world. For example, the American Ballet Theatre in New York has dancers from Cuba, Spain, Argentina, Italy, and Ukraine.

Most ballerinas are members of just one ballet company, but they dance with many others. The most famous ballerinas, such as the ones in chapter 3, have the opportunity to travel. They appear as guest ballerinas with other companies and sometimes dance in special ballets made just for them.

Keeping on Their Toes

Ballerinas first started dancing on the tips of their toes—called *en pointe* (ON PWAHNT)—in 1830. To help them do this, they wear special shoes made of satin and leather. The end of the toe is flat and has a hard block. The block is made of canvas and glue. A ballerina uses at least three pairs of shoes a week, and needs three new pairs for each performance.

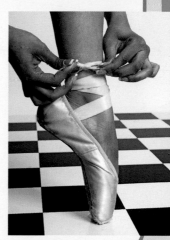

FAMOUS
Ballerinas

Ballerinas thrill fans around the world. Let's meet some of today's most well-known ballerinas.

Wendy Whelan grew up in Louisville, Kentucky. She started ballet lessons when she was three, because her mom told her it might be fun. When Wendy was 13, she took a course at the School of American Ballet in New York. At 15, she left home to study at the school full-time.

Wendy joined the New York City Ballet in 1986.

a *corps de ballet* member, she had trouble learning all the steps. She went home and wrote out pages of notes. Five years later, her hard work paid off when she was named a principal dancer.

Wendy is known for her elegant, bold dancing style.

Sylvie Guillem is a French ballerina. She started out as a gymnast, but when she was 11 she began training at the Paris Opera Ballet School. When she was 16, she joined its *corps de ballet*. She started dancing in more important roles when she was just 19.

A few years later, Sylvie left Paris to star in the Royal Ballet in London. Since then, she has performed with companies all over Europe and with the American Ballet Theatre.

Sylvie is known for being able to bend and stretch her body in strange ways. When she lifts her leg, she can touch her ear! Her flexibility and control over her body is amazing.

"Having limits to push against is how you find out what you can do," Sylvie says. "I am shy, but I love the freedom of the stage when I am dancing."

Sylvie got a special award from the British government for her beautiful dancing.

Ballerinas like Nina sometimes use things such as chairs in their dances.

Nina Ananiashvili was born in Tbilisi, Georgia (the country, not the state), where she became an ice-skating champion at the age of 10. The same year, she also started studying ballet, and decided she liked that better. When she was 13, she moved to Moscow and studied at the school of the Bolshoi Ballet, a very famous company in Russia.

Today, Nina dances with the Bolshoi Ballet and with the American Ballet Theatre. She has made guest appearances with companies all over the world, and sometimes appears in special ballets created just for her.

Nina had a baby in 2006, and has already returned to the stage to dance!

People love Nina's very elegant, dramatic style of dancing. But it's not easy to look so beautiful all the time. She says, "Of course, I'm a normal person and sometimes it's difficult because I'm in pain and you have to keep going even when you want to sleep. But when I'm on stage, I forget everything."

Tamara Rojo was born in Montreal, Canada. Her parents are Spanish, and they moved back to Spain when she was four months old. She started dancing at a Madrid dance school when she was 10 years old.

Tamara has always wanted to be a ballerina, not because she wants to be famous, but because she loves it. "You don't wish to be a a star," she says. "You just wish to dance."

When she was 20, she started dancing with the Scottish Ballet. Then she became a principal dancer with the English National Ballet, and, finally, a prima ballerina at London's Royal Ballet—the first Spanish dancer to do so.

Erica performs the Spanish Dance from the famous ballet, The Nutcracker.

In 2001, the *Chicago Sun Times* newspaper named Erica a Black History Maker. In 2003, *Ebony* magazine featured her as a Young Leader of the Future in the Arts.

Erica Lynette Edwards dances with the Joffrey Ballet in Chicago. She began dancing at age four, and went to special dance schools most of her life. While she was in college (studying dance, of course!), she won an **apprenticeship** with the director of the Joffrey Ballet. When she finished her apprenticeship, she joined the company.

Erica is from Downer's Grove, Illinois. She says she loves dancing in Chicago, which is very close to her hometown. She isn't an international star yet, but she is widely admired for her great energy and speed as a dancer.

It's fun, but it's not easy. Keep practicing like this young dancer, and maybe your ballet dreams will come true.

These wonderful ballerinas love to dance and to perform for fans like you. Maybe someday, you'll be in their shoes . . . and on their stages!

GLOSSARY

apprenticeship a time when someone learns how to do something by working with someone who already knows how to do it

audition a short performance used to test the talent of a performer

ballet a kind of entertainment in which dancers perform to music, usually to tell a story

choreographers people who create and direct the dance movements of others

corps de ballet the dancers in a ballet company who perform as a group

en pointe on the tips of the toes

flexible easy to bend

principal dancers the stars of a ballet company

professional doing something as your main job

rehearsals meetings where performers practice for a public show

scenery the painted scenes on a stage

FIND OUT MORE

BOOKS

The Ballet Book: The Young Performer's Guide to Classical Dance
by The National Ballet School of Canada (Firefly Books, 1999)
Packed with information on dance steps and poses, this great guide can even help you find a dance teacher and pick a dance school.

Becoming a Ballerina
by Susan Jaffe (Universe, 2003)
Follow a young dancer from dance classes and learning her routine to the final show.

The Illustrated Book of Ballet Stories
by Barbara Newman (Dorling Kindersley, 2005)
Learn the storylines of the five most popular ballets: *Giselle*, *Coppelia*, *Sleeping Beauty*, *The Nutcracker*, and *Swan Lake*. This book also comes with a CD of these ballets' music.

WEB SITES

Visit our Web page for lots of links about ballet and ballet dancers: www.childsworld.com/links

Note to Parents, Teachers, and Librarians: We routinely check our Web links to make sure they're safe, active sites—so encourage your readers to check them out!

INDEX

American Ballet Theater, 19, 23, 25

Ananiashvili, Nina, 24-25

ballet school, 10-11,

ballet terminology, 13, 14, 20

Bolshoi Ballet, 24-25

choreographers, 8

learning to dance, 12-13

Edwards, Erica Lynette, 28-29

English National Ballet, 27

first woman dancer, 7

Gomes, Marcelo, 18

Guillem, Sylvie, 22-23

Herrera, Paloma, 18

history, 6-7, 8-9

Joffrey Ballet, 28

Kirov Ballet, 14

Louis XIV, 7

New York City Ballet, 20

Nutcracker, The, 28

Paris Opera Ballet School, 22

Rojo, Tamara, 27

Royal Ballet, 23, 27

Russia, 24

Scottish Ballet, 27

Spain, 27

Taglioni, Maria, 6

types of dancers, 14-15

typical day, 16-17

Whelan, Wendy, 20-21

HEIDI ADELMAN has been going to the ballet since she was four years old, and she started taking lessons when she was six. She definitely wanted to be a ballerina when she grew up. Instead, she is a writer and a book editor. But she still loves to go to the ballet, and it is always a very magical experience.

J 792.8
ADEL
11/16/07
20.00